REGENTS OF
THE SEVEN SPHERES

Books by H. K. Challoner

The Wheel of Rebirth
The Path of Healing
The Sword and the Spirit

with Ronald Northover:

Antidote to Fear

The Teacher

REGENTS OF
THE SEVEN SPHERES

BY

H. K. CHALLONER

With eight colour plates

THEOSOPHICAL PUBLISHING HOUSE LONDON LTD
68 GREAT RUSSELL STREET
LONDON, W.C.1

ADYAR, INDIA   WHEATON, U.S.A

ISBN 0 7229 5009 8

PRINTED IN GREAT BRITAIN BY
FLETCHER AND SON LTD, NORWICH

REGENTS OF THE SEVEN SPHERES

FOREWORD

Watchers of the Seven Spheres—now renamed *Regents of the Seven Spheres* as more accurately expressing their nature and functions—was published over thirty years ago, therefore I feel that for those who have not previously come across the series of books written at that time (now virtually unobtainable) a few words of explanation as to the method employed to dictate them by the entity I have called the Teacher may be of interest.

As this is fully described in the first book—*The Wheel of Rebirth*—I will give here only a brief outline of the extraordinary events which culminated in my contact with him.

Several months earlier I was persuaded, very much against my will, to attend a spiritualist meeting. The medium picked me out and said that he was instructed to tell me by one he called "a guide", who was standing beside me, that I would shortly be writing under dictation a book on reincarnation and he mentioned at the same time that he saw some Egyptian hieroglyphics above my head.

As I was convinced that I did not possess any psychic powers and had only read a relatively few theosophical works at that time I was extremely sceptical. In any case, I very much disapproved of psychic practices in general and any form of automatic writing in particular, knowing the dangers of self-deception and even of obsession to which this kind of activity can lead. Also I was engaged upon other work at the time which I had no intention of dropping.

Not long after this I went to stay in a lonely bungalow by the sea with two friends, one of whom possessed a number of psychic gifts. Soon he began to see strange scenes in a crystal. Then phenomena, some of it unpleasant, started to manifest and we all became aware of a strange sense of tension as if a vortex of great power were building up. We were not so alarmed as we probably would have been had we known more about such things, although we did know that such psychic phenomena could be dangerous—as I have noted above. But somehow we seem not to have associated our experiences with any serious possibilities of that kind. The poltergeist activities which are often a side effect of the building up of power we merely considered to be rather a joke.

One night I had a vivid dream of myself as a man in Atlantis. It broke off abruptly but the next night was resumed in much more detail although it was still left unfinished. I had a powerful impulse somehow to learn the end of the story and was the more easily persuaded to try and see if I could get anything through in automatic writing, despite my ideas on the subject and the fact that I was sure it would be no use. But after one or two failures in company with the other two, who clearly helped to contribute the power, information began to come through from someone who claimed to be a dead relative of all three of us and who again reiterated that a "teacher" wished to write a book by using my hand if I was prepared to co-operate with him.

At first I was very dubious, but when, eventually, the teacher himself made contact with us and I became aware of the amazing vibration of peace, love and wisdom which accompanied his presence I was completely reassured and became eager to go on with the experiment.

This sense of security and "rightness" was increased when I realized that there was no question of my going into trance, no compulsion would be exercised at any time, and, whereas at the beginning, the control was very powerful and I was trained to react to the least pressure or impulse so that my hands seemed not to be my own, this decreased as I got used to the method and it soon developed into a form of close co-operation as between two people working together almost with one mind.

I cannot say, even now, the exact nature of the technique which the teacher employed when dictating the actual episodes of my past in the *Wheel of Rebirth* and, much more important, the explanations of the working of the law and the other teachings which followed them. It seemed to consist in a form of mental telepathy by means of which his ideas were impressed upon my brain. I was always aware of what was to be written before it came through in a handwriting which was entirely different from my own.

The nearest thing to which I can liken it is inspiration, when words and images pour into the writing, in particular of poetry and occasionally in a novel; although in this case it was much more powerful and vivid. Later, drawings and paintings were given in a rather similar way but here the control was stronger. This was even more impressive to me as they mostly consisted of figures and were very beautiful, whereas it would have been absolutely impossible for me to draw the human figure with any degree of accuracy for I was not a trained artist. The process rather resembled one in which an artist might endeavour to guide the hand of a child.

During all this time I was being given intensive training and instruction and knew almost from minute to minute what I was supposed to do; but I was always left completely free and could break off the contact at any time. Also I could ask questions, argue or frankly disagree. This is an extremely important point, because any kind of control which interferes in the slightest degree with the free will of the subject should be suspect. That is the method used by the forces of darkness.

Eventually, however, the contact grew more tenuous and distant as if the teacher were gradually going further away, as indeed was the case. For after a time he informed me that soon he would withdraw altogether from this close association because it was essential that I should learn to use all I had been taught in practical application to daily living and continue the disciplines without any external help. He pointed out that it was neither desirable nor even permissible that anyone should have knowledge, wisdom and above all direction imposed, as it were, from the outside beyond a certain point. The real aim was for us to acquire ourselves the ability to "enter into the silence", that is to say, invoke the wisdom of the "Master in the heart", that point of divinity possessed by all men which is sometimes called the Higher Self or the Soul, the seat of divine wisdom. This must eventually be the only guide of every individual who aspires towards the Light, and such a true alignment can never be achieved save by our own efforts.

The sceptic, and above all the psychiatrist, will no doubt decide that the whole experience was some kind of projection from the unconscious, a wish-fulfilment fantasy or simply that I was suffering from mental aberrations.

But do such people really know what the unconscious or subconscious mind really is? The great psychiatrist,

Jung, postulates that there exist whole areas in our total economy which extend far beyond even the personal life. These areas may well include not only the vast realms of what he has named the collective unconscious, that is the whole field of race memory, but may even be the store-house of personal memories of our own long journey through time from the remote past. Occasionally the latter have been resurrected during the dangerous process of deep analysis and have been known to cause disturbances with which the practitioner has been quite unable to deal.

There is also the superconscious or soul level. Upon this the average man hardly if ever functions, at least during his day-time activities, although its influence may profoundly affect him without his knowledge.

This area may well extend far upward or outward and be reinforced by relationships with other souls at similar or even higher levels still since the soul is group-conscious. Thus we can be put into contact with entities far more advanced than ourselves, and by association with them, can draw upon their knowledge and wisdom.

In certain conditions, because of the need for some work which those who seek to help the human race and are its guardians and teachers wish to see carried out, creative ideas far beyond the normal capacity of limited human powers to acquire can be transmitted to us in this way, and so-called flashes of inspiration, new discoveries and concepts useful to humanity are projected into minds which are sufficiently attuned and open to register them.

.   .   .   .

It was before the teacher withdrew altogether that, for a brief period, I was put into contact with beings of a very different order—the deva or angelic kingdom. In this book I have used the Eastern term, deva, as being the most convenient one since it includes all grades of beings from the very greatest to the smallest, nor has it acquired a wrong and often debased image as that from materialistic representations of angels in Churches, books and paintings from earlier times has done.

The phase was a brief one but during this period the poems and pictures reproduced here were precipitated through my hand.

I was staying at that time in the country—indeed, clearly, it is only in solitary places close to nature that any such contact would be possible. And as I walked in woods and fields it was as if their radiant presences filled earth and sky and their voices spoke soundlessly in my ears. Although I never saw them as a clairvoyant might have done, I seemed to feel them so vividly that their forms became known to me, and I could tell beforehand what my pencil and brush would produce; although it hardly seems necessary to say that nothing could hope to depict their splendour, the shining light and almost unearthly colours which surrounded them, nor, above all, the atmosphere of radiant joy combined with creative power which they emanated.

Here it may be as well to explain something of the nature of the Deva kingdom for those who may not have previously read much about it, although both in the teacher's talk and in the poems themselves a great deal of information is given.

In order to understand and to be able to accept the fact that there exists in our universe this great company of unseen beings, we must first have some slight idea—it cannot clearly be more than that—of the total plan or pattern upon which the whole system of evolution is constructed, from that of the inconceivable vastness of an island universe to the tiny world of the atom.

This is the Hierarchical System—the outer reflection of the intrinsic unity existing throughout all manifestation. The concept is set forth with the greatest possible lucidity in the famous axiom attributed to Hermes Trismegistus and is an accepted part of the teaching of the Mystery Schools.

As it is Above so it is below;
As it is Within so it is without;
As in the Great so in the small;
There is but one Life and one Law.

The simplest way to perceive this law of hierarchy in operation is by first looking at the "below"—our own world.

From our day to day experience we know that any organization, in order to be efficient, must be based upon this hierarchical system. That is to say it must have a head, one who inaugurates the guiding principles which it is designed to express and which those below him carry out.

This functional pattern has existed in all living combinations from the very earliest times.

First came the family unit with the parents at its head and children and servants below them in authority. In the tribe it was the same with a chief or high priest whom all obeyed. As complexity increased and states and nations came into being, a king or later a president stood as a symbol of the central power with, in descending order, his ministers and those who carried out their orders and so on downward. It is even reflected in the animal and insect world where the individual is part of a group. There is a leader of the herd or pack, even a pecking order in hens, and the most perfect example of the system, as such, is clearly exemplified in the life of the hive and the ant-heap.

One thing is worth noting: when any human society attempts to build itself upon any other principle—such as that of absolute equality between all the members—invariably in time the basic pattern reasserts itself and dominant figures begin to emerge. We cannot get away from this external manifestation of an inner universal law.

But what is equally significant is that we find it also governing the constitution of matter, in the world of space and in that of the atom. There is always a centre—such as the sun—with his planets, or the cell with its nucleus; that is, a point of power which gives life and energy to the whole of the structure.

I have begun with a rather sketchy presentation of the system as it works below or in the outer because this is so obvious to us and so familiar, but, as we have seen, according to this system of thought the outer is only a reflection in matter of the Above and the Within—that is to say the spiritual world which exists above, within or behind (all words in essence false but which we, governed as we are by the concepts of space and time cannot avoid) the physical plane and which corresponds in certain aspects to Plato's concept of the world of archetypes or divine ideas.

It is taught in the Ancient Wisdom, which comprises the basic concepts to be found in the great world-wide Mystery religions of which all exoteric faiths are the outer form stepped down to meet the mentality of the average man, that everything in existence is the objective appearance of a spiritual "being". This applies equally to the universe itself, the "garment" of God Immanent, every constellation, galaxy, quasar, sun and planet down to the smallest particle of matter. All and each are representative of aspects of the manifestation of divine energy or the all-pervasive Life of God.

It follows, therefore, that what the average man believes to be merely masses of matter or gas are, in actual fact, the "bodies of expression" of great Intelligences all evolving, as everything else in manifestation evolves, through utilizing the energies, powers and expanding capacities of those lesser beings which form part of their specific mode of growth, just as the cells in our body are essential to our own.

This incalculable host of beings who fill the universe, and of which only a relatively few possess bodies which can be perceived by our instruments, are all seeking, just as we are doing, to increase their wisdom and power, develop new insights and, to an ever greater extent, demonstrate in the universe the qualities of divinity. They might perhaps be thought of as the creative emissaries to all those below them of the divine Will to be and to become at every level of manifestation, a process which could surely continue "to no end".

If we can try for a moment to stretch imagination to the uttermost, we may gain a faint flash of realization implied by the words of a sage: "There is no being in the universe so great that a greater cannot be conceived."

A.E. the mystic and poet gives us a marvellous picture of the cosmos alive with these mighty Powers when, in *The House of the Titans* he writes of:—

... The High Grandees,
The very noblest of the universe,
Princes of stars and solar kings and rulers
Of constellations and of galaxies ...

The existence of this hierarchy of beings has always been recognized in one form or another by virtually every religious system down the ages. In the pagan world the higher devas were worshipped as gods, and man projected upon them, as always happens, the qualities, good and bad, of his own species. It has been truly said: "God first made man in his image, but man has been returning the compliment ever since."

Christianity borrowed a great deal from the pagan world as it did from the Hebrews, and the devas became the angelic hosts. In Christian terminology the greatest of these were called Powers and Dominions, Thrones, Aeons, Cherubim and Seraphim, Angels, Archangels and all the company of heaven.

Unfortunately, although the Roman and Eastern Orthodox churches still retain a very real and living belief in their existence and invoke their powers, as witness the instructions given to a body of pilgrims by Pope Pius XII to "awaken your realization of the invisible world around you", the Reformed Churches seem almost entirely to have lost any genuine conception of their livingness and their power to aid humanity, and give them no more than lip service in a few hymns and affirmations empty of all real significance to the average Christian and, one fears, even to the average Churchman. This is a great disaster, for they are agents of immense power, creative energy and intelligence who, under direction of their Lord, could, if we knew how to approach and invoke them, help us to initiate more quickly upon earth the purposes of heaven.

Part of our trouble is, of course, that we have become so steeped in materialism that few of us can conceive of any beings who do not reside in gross physical bodies. Yet the scientists with their electronmicroscopes should have taught us that so much which is "real" in a most vital sense is invisible to us because of the limitations of our sight. The subtle ethers of which the bodies of the majority of the devas are formed could not be perceived by even more delicate instruments.

That is why, even if we do succeed in landing on other planets, it is highly unlikely that we shall see their inhabitants or their dwellings unless they deliberately make themselves known to us—which, in view of our present primitive stage of evolution and the dangers we would bring into their worlds, seems highly unlikely.

This book is naturally only concerned with those devas who inhabit our own solar system, of which the high Entity who is its centre and head is the Solar Lord and might be said to hold in his system a position analogous to that of the nucleus of life at the centre of the cell. Since the actual physical sun is his body of manifestation, his radiations give life and energy to all his "children", the planets within his sphere of influence and to all the lives upon them.

Thus he is *our* true "Father-in-Heaven". This was recognized by the many religions of old in which the sun was worshipped. But whereas the people actually worshipped the objective solar orb the priests and initiates knew perfectly well the truth which its appearance hid.

But we must not forget that our Solar Lord is himself the reflection or child of Another, his own Lord or Ruler, of whose "body" he is an aspect, in the same way as the planetary Regents are aspects of his; and he, like them, is the recipient of as much of the power, glory and divine wisdom mediated down to him as he is capable of assimilating.

Below him are his ministers and servants, the deva hosts, from great Intelligences down to tiny unself-conscious beings, all playing their part in carrying out his will which is to achieve perfection relative to his present limitations in his whole economy from highest to lowest in accordance with the Law, so that he and all the lives which are emanations from his life may progress into higher states of being. For until all are "saved", that is to say redeemed from the illusion of their separateness and the thraldom imposed upon them by ignorance, he himself cannot pass on to higher stages of evolution.

In this very brief and inevitably superficial picture, we can perceive the resemblance between the development of the greater Lives and our own. *There is but one Life and one Law.* But it also touches upon one of the deep mysteries of cosmic life, that of sacrifice by means of mediation or transmission of power from one level to the next. This must inevitably imply some measure of self-limitation and diminishment, hence in a very esoteric sense, of suffering. Of this process the Christ was the supreme symbol in our world.

It is taught that the devas both outside our system as well as within it are essentially the builders of the universe, those who hold form in coherent shape, transmuting, applying and circulating the pranic emanations within their specific sphere of influence. They build in etheric matter, each group or kingdom conforming always to the hierarchical pattern, so that there are

Lords of fire and fire elementals, similarly of air, water and earth. All these have also their correspondences, of course, in the realms of emotion, mind and spirit.

The lesser beings, the nature spirits, obey the creative impulses coming from those whose task it is to direct them. Their existence is no longer believed in by modern man and they only live on in the beliefs of primitive peoples and in fairy-tale and folk-lore as gnomes in the earth, elves, fairies and undines of hills, woods, fields and streams, salamanders in the fire. Being unselfconscious and not yet possessing a soul they are entirely amoral and obey the commands of anyone who knows how to stimulate them to activity. Many human beings do this quite unconsciously, wielding powers through their agency of which they are themselves unaware. A good example of this is the possession of "green fingers". Such people probably use magnetic attraction or love of nature and understanding of her laws; for the elementals are drawn to any who "sound their note", that is set up a vibration in harmony with their own.

It is interesting in this connection to note that in many fairy stories the fairy seeks to "marry" a mortal in order to enter the human kingdom and so acquire a soul, that is to say, become a self-conscious being and take the next upward step in evolution. Some people believe that many creative and amoral types in our world may well be the first incarnation of devas not much higher than those of the elemental order. It is also significant to find how often birds enter into these stories and legends, acting as messengers and helpers of mankind, for there is a belief that some of the lower elemental beings occasionally enter the bird kingdom on their way towards that of the human.

Is it also significant that in our day, possibly for the first time, a particular interest in and care for the bird and animal kingdom (actually they are one) is becoming so widespread? The closer association of human and animal, often amounting to friendship and love on both sides, could well be another indication of the speeding up of the evolutionary process which we see taking place in so many fields of activity through discovery, experimentation and experience.

This applies equally to the ability to make contact with the greater beings for it is the basis of magic. Sound, scent, colour, movement all set up certain vibrations at subtler levels and if the right correspondences are known these can be used to attract specific devas—hence the whole art of ceremonial.

Needless to say the greater devas only respond to vibrations of love and work with those who seek to implement the laws of God. But the lower ones, while doing likewise, can also be commanded by practitioners of black magic who know how to direct their activities by the use of the will and knowledge of the means relating to their specific modes of response.

It is said that devas and men evolve through interaction with each other and that whereas man is *innately* love—the force which produces coherency—the devas are innately intelligence, the force which produces activity.

There is no doubt that numbers of legends about the activities of the gods as well as many fairy-stories originated in an attempt to inculcate truths by the use of parables and pictures into the minds of the uneducated masses, just as Jesus did, but they are full of symbolism for those who can interpret them. Indeed they often possess as much as three levels of meaning, revealing deeps upon deeps. This, indeed, is equally true of the actual forms and energies in the natural world. For instance, the elements as we know them are the reflection in matter of their higher counterparts, energies and forces which become materialized at the lower levels through the agency of the devas.

It seems possible, indeed, that if destructive currents of emotional energy generated by humanity become powerful enough, they might even be instrumental in stimulating the corresponding elemental life into such violent activity that phenomena such as hurricanes, tempests and even earthquakes could eventuate. For we are one with our earth at every level.

One thing is important to keep in mind when trying to understand these kingdoms above and below the human level: no explanations or interpretations must ever be taken too literally or believed implicitly. A scripture says: *Nothing is true, nothing is false. All things are but masks of truth.*[1] Everything in our world has a deeper interpretation at a more inward or esoteric level. The more we learn, and the more we realize this the more we try to keep an open mind and cease entirely to make dogmatic assertions about anything.

This is particularly relevant to the forms in which the devas in this book have been depicted. All form is illusory in the sense that it is, in essence, an expression of or projection made upon receptive human faculties and can be modified or even changed up to a point by the particular ideas, prejudices or interests of the observer. A sunset seen through the eyes of an artist, a farmer, a scientist, or the average unobservant man would have

---

[1] *The Sayings of the Ancient One.* P. G. Bowen. Rider & Co.

an entirely different significance—or none. Forms are, in one sense always symbolical of activities beyond themselves.

So far as the devas are concerned this is borne out by the fact that, according to his traditions and the land in which he lives, the psychic sees the devas, high or low, within his own particular frame of reference. He projects upon the impression he receives of an immaterial being the images he thinks it should take. Thus, the Indian devas are represented in forms corresponding to Indian beliefs and have Indian-type faces; the Greeks humanized their gods and gave them perfect human bodies and human characteristics. In the Western Christian world angels and fairies have wings and the nature spirits, gnomes and elves are still depicted with human shapes in miniature.

Man cannot escape the forms which are familiar to him; all he can do is to distort and change them by exaggeration or diminution.

No doubt to themselves and to each other the devas appear utterly different from anything we can imagine, certainly they do not possess human form. Why should they?

Being centres of energy they are said to manifest as whirling spheres of light, colour and sound combined, many dimensional and ever-changing with every impulse or thought they register. Moreover their colours and the sounds they give forth must, for the most part, be far beyond the limits our human senses could register.

It may be asked: why, then, do they appear in these pictures with human faces and human hands?

The answer, I think, is that how otherwise could we get any ideas about them at all? If it were possible, which clearly it never could be, to depict them as they are, the effect would convey little or nothing to the observer.

So certain parts of the human form have been used in order to convey symbolically the powers and attributes of the devas in question.

Now the agents for the expression of power in our bodies are chiefly the eye, the mouth and the hand: that is to say vision, sound and creativity. So they have shown themselves as possessing human eyes in an idealized human face with, in some cases, human hands. It is worth noting that the heart centre always appears as an active agent of light and force because this is the seat of divine love, consequently of the Life Force itself, and it is from this centre that streams of light and energy are radiated into their environment. The aspect of one or two may appear to us terrible or remote; this is to create the *impression* of the specific aspect of power of which such groups of devas are lord.

. . . .

As regards the portrait, I have been asked why the eyes are downcast or appear to be closed. After much thought I have come to the conclusion that it may be that, as this book is to go out to the general public, certain people with more ardour than understanding might try to use the picture for meditation purposes before they are ready, occultly speaking, to make direct contact with the teacher.

As pointed out in connection with the devas, the eyes are important agents for the projection of power, as hypnotism has proved. Thus, if he were gazing for any length of time directly into the eyes of such a portrait, the aspirant could induce in himself an auto-hypnotic state or receive a greater impact from such contemplation than was safe or desirable.

But there is another possibility. There is an ancient axiom: *When the pupil is ready the Master appears.* For those who, unprepared, attempt through excessive devotion, the exercise of the will or under the urge of what is simply vanity, to make direct contact with a teacher on the inner planes, the effort can be not merely futile (which would not matter so much) but exceedingly dangerous. This is particularly the case when the motives are not absolutely pure and arise from the emotional level rather than the mental discriminative faculty. For often what may seem to the aspirant to be pure devotion can easily be tainted by less admirable qualities.

Efforts empowered by the wrong motives can easily attract an evil or foolish entity wandering on the astral planes who will masquerade as a teacher or even a Master of Wisdom, actually taking on the appropriate appearance to those who are clairvoyant, for it is said that the astral plane—which we must remember is a plane of illusion, just as the physical plane is—is full of thought-forms of Masters which are no more than shells created by the blind passionate desire of devotees. These can easily be appropriated by some lower entity who, like a will-o'-the-wisp, will end by leading the unfortunate deluded one ever deeper into the mire.

On the other hand when some *aspect* of an aspirant can be used to put out teaching, contact at one level or another may be made. This does not mean that the aspirant, as a whole man, need be very advanced. I, certainly, was anything but that; in fact, as I have pointed out earlier, I had hardly begun to study these subjects and certainly had done no meditation exercises.

In fact I should have said I was entirely unsuitable for such work. But in cases such as this, presumably influences from the past, tasks undertaken in previous lives and contacts made then would be taken into consideration.

In any case, one thing is certain, any such contact must be initiated by the teacher himself in the right and safe way. The person approached will also always be given free choice in the matter. Any undue pressure, any appeal to vanity, above all the exercise of any compulsion should be instantly suspect. This is not the way the teachers on the Right Hand Path ever work.

But if anyone desires to serve and further the effort always being made from spiritual levels to teach and help mankind there is one sure way he can prepare himself to do so, as the teacher himself tells us. This is by serving *where he already stands* and using all means in his power to clear the channels between the lower personality and the Higher Self—the Soul. For this is the doorway into the realms where teachers and greater beings ever await that moment when the note is sounded which tells them that among the millions of men who know them not, one more aspirant is ready to enter the Stream. And then, when the call comes, as come it surely will in one form or another, we shall be prepared to answer it.

.   .   .   .   .

One more comment may be of interest. It could be especially significant that this book is being reissued at this time. It is said that: "only that which is timely is right" and it is certainly true that many discoveries, experiments and even revelations which have been made when there was not sufficient response in humanity to accept, even less to attempt to implement them, have failed or gone underground, as it were, awaiting their time to re-emerge. An example of this is to be found in the life of Akhnaton whose teachings were of pure love leading even to a refusal to kill his enemies; in many other ways they were very close to the teachings of Jesus. But the world was not ready even to consider them at that time. When Jesus came at least a nucleus existed which was.

In our day there seems to be the beginning of a revival of interest and even belief in the existence of immaterial beings. There have been numbers of reports that people, not normally clairvoyant, have claimed to see great Presences in the air; and "flying saucers" are accepted as a reality by very many thoughtful and intelligent folk. Though whether they are materialized forms of beings who wish to make us realize that we are not alone in our own system, let alone in the universe, and not space craft at all, does not seem to have occurred to the majority.

Certainly the growing acceptance of the possible existence of extra-terrestial beings by the public, owing to space exploration and the statements by astronomers that many other suns may have planets in which conditions similar to ours exist, is yet another factor in this more general awakening; as is also the popularity of such books as those by Raynor Johnson, in particular *Nurslings of Immortality*, in which he introduces to the public the works of the poet-philosopher, Douglas Fawcett and his theory of the existence of the Imaginals, a Divine Society of great creative Intelligences, clearly but another term for the higher devas and those advanced beings associated with them.

There seems also, in this country at least, to be a revival of an awareness of the importance of the influence of the great Archangel, Michael. By many esoterists he is believed to be the real guardian angel of Britain, the prototype of St. George who is a popular conception of him and represents, in the public imagination, some of his specific attributes, such as killing the dragon, symbol of evil, and rescuing the maiden who, of course, is a symbol of the human soul.

This movement towards a growing awareness of the angelic or deva kingdoms may well be the result of an attempt by the teachers of the race to awaken the public to the importance of co-operation with this great hierarchy, many of whom are said to be only awaiting recognition in order to be enabled to be of greater service to mankind. It could also be part of the preparation for the new Age and the tremendous influx of new energies, accompanied by a spiritual revival, prophesied for the end of this century as an essential step to the preparation of humanity for a fresh downpouring of the Christ spirit on earth.

One of the aspects which, it is said, will be predominant in the Age of Aquarius will be an entirely new form of *conscious* co-operation between humanity and the devic forces; the constructive and inspirational energies of mankind will be drawn into ever closer alignment with the creative sources of life, which will help stimulate our imaginative faculties and give us a far greater and more all-inclusive vision of the divine Plan.

Hitherto much that has come to us from these higher realms has done so from sources of which we are not conscious, such as those flashes which we sometimes get on waking or when we are seeking solutions to important problems; but in future inspiration will have to be deliberately invoked in entirely new ways and with an entirely new understanding of the real processes involved.

Man will then begin to learn how to practice what is, in essence, a form of white magic, discovering what specific sounds and what appropriate colours and movements should be employed in order to attract the devic forces to aid him in his work for humanity.

It is also significant in this connection that numbers of scientists, hitherto sceptical of all so-called "occult" or esoteric teachings, are moving, almost in spite of themselves, ever nearer to acceptance of the existence of great, as yet undeveloped potentialities in man, such as extrasensory perception in its numerous forms.

It may indeed be from the discoveries of science rather than from the Church that the religion for the new Age will emerge, for it is in part such discoveries as the above that are being instrumental in breaking up the hard, crystallized shell of dogma, false assumptions and outmoded beliefs which have hitherto prevented any real progress in the evolution of organized religion. This is happening already with a surprising momentum, as witness the stream of books critical of the present attitudes regarding religion being written by bishops, clergy and many laymen who take the subject seriously and realize the desperate need for reform which could regenerate society.

In his foreword the teacher has himself enlarged on many of the themes touched on in this preface, and the devas, through his mediation, have described their nature, their activities and their aims.

But it cannot be emphasized too often that no human words can express the inner significance of such work as theirs, which can only be revealed still deeply veiled by man's own limitations.

Yet the intuitive reader may glimpse something here that may give him insight into those great forces which are in process of endeavouring to turn to constructive ends the apparent chaos of our time and are even using our confusion and despair for the furtherance of the Divine Plan.

.   .   .   .

REGENTS OF THE SEVEN SPHERES

I

THE TEACHER SPEAKS

"He who desires to prove for himself the existence of the Shining Ones—angels, devas, gods, call them by whatsoever name you will—he who would hear the sweetness of their voices, see their bright shapes moving at their appointed tasks in perfect harmony with the Will which called them and all things forth into manifestation; he who would understand the laws of their being and would co-operate in their divine activities, let him learn to lift his consciousness above the conflicting and deceptive forms, changing illusions of stability, which torment the dweller in the world of sense. Let him seek that sphere where light and sound, in their infinitely changing shapes and patterns, reflect, as in a lake's still, midday surface, the flawless image of the Thought Divine.

"Here, unruffled by the capricious winds of emotion, he will perceive that which is hidden from those who as yet care not to know what is, what has been and what shall be. Here he will learn to comprehend laws only revealed to those who, desiring truth above all else, focus their energies one-pointedly upon its attainment, and are willing to risk, to this end, the loss of all things that the world holds most dear.

"Yet do not think, O you who desire Sight, Vision and Knowledge, that easily—or in one life—can these be attained. Long and hard is the path; yet it must be

31

trodden, not by a few alone but by the majority of men, if the human race is to reach those supreme heights of glory and achievement to which, in his noblest moments, man aspires.

"The age of such perfected and divine humanity, in harmony with itself and with all creation, is still infinitely remote; but that age will come, and it is for you, children of this present age of transition, to thrust open once again the doors to the Temple of Truth that the materialism of past centuries has kept so rigorously closed, and to take the first steps toward the light therein enshrined which will reveal to those who dare approach it how this union of men and of devas, without which a greater revelation of nature's laws will ever be impossible, may be more speedily brought about.

"But before this can be done it is essential that man should acknowledge the existence of the Deva Hierarchy, those beings who are, in fact, the personification of all energy and of every element which enters into the manifestation of form. For Life, in its entirety, is deva essence. Man lives unceasingly in their emanations, although he knows it not; his work in the coming centuries is to discover how he may live consciously with them in knowledge and understanding.

"Once, long ago, men and devas did so dwell together in unity, but the memory of that age is obscured by the mists of legend and lingers alone in the myths and the fairy tales of the race.

"And as for centuries to mankind in general the deva kingdom has been invisible and even unknown, so save for the more enlightened who have become clairvoyant to the physical plane as some men have to the astral, the devas have ignored individual man, sensing him only as a

cloud of light or a burst of music, a vibration harmonious
or otherwise according to his nature.

"For to them all is vibration. It is their language, and
their key-note. They dwell in a realm of ecstatic beauty
and love, a realm of music visible in glittering, transient
shapes, of colour audible in waves of exquisite sound; of
perpetually whirling atoms of matter, changing, coales-
cing, separating in response to the propulsions of the
creative energy which the devas themselves live solely to
express.

"Thus only when man himself seeks to manifest the
divine power of creation and, through an effort of will or
by the force of love, gives forth a strong desire to build in
mind or in matter, do they become aware of him. When
this occurs those devas attuned to whatever note he
sounds are drawn irresistibly towards him and remain
caught within the vortex of energy he has generated,
continuing to play their vitalizing force upon it until the
primary impulse fades or the form is completed.

"It follows then, that it is for man consciously to
approach the devas, if he desires to be instrumental in
bringing about this new contact between the two kingdoms and to work with the divine plan for the evolution
of the coming race.

"For at the inception of every new age in the history
of mankind Those who control and guide the govern-
ment of the inner worlds inaugurate some special line of
development whereby all beings will be enabled to
acquire new powers which will give them insight into the
as yet unrevealed aspects of the One Truth.

"To this end a great outpouring of spiritual energy is
vouchsafed in order to stimulate the higher bodies of all
who are capable of response. So it is at the present time.

Those who are ready to co-operate with this aspect of the divine Plan will have for their especial work to strive to open men's eyes to the wonders of the Deva Kingdom and thus to hasten the day when man will recognize their existence and their power to aid him. For, as the number of men who learn to speak their language increases, many devas will, through this closer contact, come themselves more clearly to apprehend the problems of those manifesting in dense material conditions.

"In consequence of this increased understanding they will be enabled to take a still more active part in man's struggle to synthesize his bodies and gain greater harmony both within and without, and help and inspire him in all his activities.

"Many at a lower level may, indeed, by reason of the close sympathy which will in time develop between individual members of the two kingdoms, be drawn into the human world and take human bodies.

"Already, although the New Age is but in its inception, great waves of force, more especially from the Sign Aquarius, which will have a very important influence on the new race type, have been released to play upon the earth. The effect of this influx of energy will become more and more apparent as time goes on and new generations, attuned to its particular rate of vibration, are born. With this regenerating force, which will affect every part of man, will come, inevitably, hosts of Aquarian devas; for each deva kingdom is affiliated with a particular type of force emanating from one of the Zodiacal signs.

"These devas and many more from Sagittarius and other signs closely connected with the building and preparing of the races of the future, will be the divine messengers, pouring into the hearts and minds of men unaccustomed thoughts, hopes and aspirations.

"Their work can already be discerned. The search for new forms of self-expression in art and in life; the discoveries in the realms of science and in psychology; the increasing effort man is making to lift the veil from the unseen worlds and to apprehend truth with fourth dimensional vision; all these are but the reflection on earth of the activities upon the inner planes of these Builders of the New Age, who are ceaselessly impressing man's mind with the desire to acquire faculties he has not yet, but which it is their particular work to develop within him.

"In all ages throughout the whole of the evolution of humanity such work has been in progress, but each new age demands new methods; and through a complete re-orientation of outlook alone can the modern man hope to bring about these changes which will mean so much to him.

"At this present time many seers of the race, responding to the particular influence of devas from the Sign Pisces which has now governed the world for many centuries, still seek, as have done the mystics of the past, through devotion to still the mind and listen to inner voices. But the age of Pisces is waning; its devas are already being withdrawn before the invasion of those new forces of which I spoke, and man, swept forward upon these advancing waves of cosmic energy, is becoming ever more and more positive; he demands action, speed, mental efficiency in every branch of his activities. No longer content to listen to the voice of tradition or to the pronouncements of others, he wills to experiment—to become himself the KNOWER. Those, therefore, who would be the seers and spiritual leaders of this coming race will have, perforce, to learn how they may, through personal knowledge and control, attain to the understanding of and participation in the working of the laws of nature which this closer contact with the Deva Hierarchy will gradually reveal to any who are willing to study its mysteries.

"For man stands indeed upon the threshold of discoveries, of revelations, of the attainment of powers never before known, not even in the days of the Atlantean Race.

"And herein lies his danger. Unless, this time, he is morally strong enough to control these forces and develops that spirituality of outlook essential to all those who wield great power, once again he will be overwhelmed; once again he will be swept to destruction by the very forces which are designed to be his benefactors.

"It is from this, the fell fruit of his own ignorance and pride, that we seek to protect him; and it is to this end that I desire to reveal to you some of the difficulties which must be faced and overcome if man is to learn to contact the devas with impunity.

"For again I would stress that the devas respond to the creative vibration a man gives forth, to the Note of Will or of Love or of Activity that he sounds upon the aeolian harp of the inner worlds. As his motives are, so will his note manifest there, either in harmony or in discord; in floods of exquisite colour or suffused with the crude shades of his own aura—and according to this Note will be the type of the devas he attracts to himself.

"And herein lies the key to the dangers which attend this fusion of human and deva; for although both are united in aim and are proceeding towards one goal, their natures are utterly unlike. The devas are not possessed, as is man, of a sense which differentiates between right and wrong; therefore, because of their very nature, void of error, or of the possibility thereof, those who function on the lower planes of the Astral and Etheric can be used by man for good or for ill.

"Only the man possessed of a clear understanding of the fundamental laws of nature can, therefore, hope to invoke the devas with safety. For if anyone should attempt so to do before he has learned a great measure of control over his emotional and mental bodies, under the tremendous outpouring of force which his invocation will draw upon him he may easily be overpowered and driven eventually to what men, in their ignorance, misname madness.

"This is one of the most common causes of the tragedy of so many of those sensitive and gifted people who possess some of the powers of genius, but lack its higher attributes. With mighty, one-pointed will the man invokes the creative energies; the devas rush in; he opens himself to them promiscuously, to the lowest as to the highest, knowing not how to discriminate between them. For a while he sees through devic eyes, hears through their immortal ears, is the recipient of some little of their knowledge, becomes forgetful of all the limitations of time and the conventional laws of less gifted men. But when the impulse slackens and the devic forces withdraw, he finds himself mentally and emotionally an empty, abandoned shell, yet still possessed of a residue of the creative energy uncorrelated within him. He who, even if unconsciously, has been trained in control, would know by instinct how to raise this surplus force from the solar plexus—through which most of the devic energy is poured—to the higher centres, but the average man will be helpless and allow the force to flood his lower centres, thus causing terrible unbalance, emotional stress and often acute sexual disturbance.

"This type of man lives ever in a world of extremes, of sudden ecstasy, of misery and despair. If then he be by nature weak, feeling himself abandoned by the stimulating influences which give him joy, he will begin to invoke those lower elemental entities who cannot function in the higher centres, and will often by them be driven to excess and degradation.

'Equally, should any seek to use the devas with deliberate intent for selfish or destructive purpose, let him beware! Eventually the result will be disaster; for the note he sounds will be a discordant one, setting up a dissonance with the creative note of the divine Will; upon this false relationship the deva essence will vibrate with greater and greater momentum until the man can no longer control it. Gradually the increasing vibration will begin to disintegrate his bodies until finally they will be destroyed by paralysis, apoplexy, or by the slower process of some cancerous disease. Finally—I say: this may not happen in one life. Be it known to you that those who in Atlantis and even in later times thus trafficked with the devas, have been forced to re-incarnate with the discord which they themselves created sounding still within them. Vibrating ever upon their etheric matter it causes ill-health, disease or death according to its strength and their own weakness. It must eventually be transmuted by the man himself into harmony through service and through love; and he is ready to be 'cured' only when his note peals forth once more in unison with the divine purpose.

"Nor have these powers been perverted to base usage in the past alone; still in some Indian cults and in the depraved rites of savages, who have retained half-forgotten fragments of the old Mysteries, the lower elemental forms are called into activity by the rhythmic beat of drums and the shrill, reiterated notes of primitive instruments. Yet worse, by far, is their invocation through the ceremonial rites and secret magic of certain religious organizations who seek, by means of devic energy, to enslave their adherents to their will by playing upon their uncontrolled emotions and ignorant fears. To these, the more enlightened, will come retribution, terrible and swift, when the hour strikes for the new outpouring of Love to flood the world with light and to open blinded eyes.

"Yet it cannot be emphasized too often that only the lower devas can thus be used for personal ends; those who are spiritually evolved would never respond to any vibration save that vitalized by pure love and intent to serve the divine Plan. They respond only to a note sounded upon their own wavelength, and to no worker on the Left Hand Path would this be revealed. It is therefore only those who have qualified to receive these secrets and are utterly dedicated who would have the power thus to attract and communicate with them.

"Therefore again I say unto you, let none attempt to make these contacts until he has proved himself fitted so to do. I may seem, perhaps, to repeat this particular warning too persistently, but I know full well how prone are men to ignore or immediately to forget any particular aspect of truth which they do not wish to believe or to which some secret part of them is in resistance. But this aspect of which I speak cannot with impunity be ignored or forgotten, and for that reason alone I stress it, as do the devas themselves.

"Remember therefore my words and meditate thereon.

"Understanding and control of the bodies is the road; love and service the bridge which leads across the gulf separating the two Kingdoms still.

"For love is the vibration to which all nature responds; it is the key-note of creation. To every outpouring of selfless love the devas answer joyfully, entering the man who loves, increasing his power with their own. All men may invoke these messengers of the divine regenerative powers in safety who strive to develop the perfect rhythm within themselves through perpetual watchfulness, love and service: for by such efforts inevitably they make contact with the creative energies through the medium of the God within their own hearts. This is the only safe way, for then he will not fail to sound the note of the devas and use it aright. He is now one with them in essence, another living and conscious spark from the One Flame.

"Therefore those who feel burning within them an ardent desire to work henceforth towards this glorious goal of union between devas and mankind, let them press forward, fearing nothing yet realizing too the magnitude of their task.

"The first step, which is often the most difficult, is for the aspirant to face *himself*; he must learn to know the real man he is, his weaknesses, his strengths and above all his many self-deceptions. Only when this has been to some extent achieved will he be capable of judging with detachment whether his motives are pure, untinged by vanity, delusion or desire for self-aggrandizement and decide whether in truth he is equipped for the sacrifices which are certain to be demanded of him.

"This step accomplished, he has to build for himself through much patient practice, bodies which, if not in this life then in the next, will enable him to do the work to which he aspires. Men are too bound by the thraldom of time and do not realize what a relatively small, though still an important part, one life plays in the continuous process of development which those with vision see as the flowing of a river towards its source.

In order to begin building the right kind of body, both sensitive and well balanced which the divine powers can impress and use to work God's purpose on earth, the man must learn to redirect his energies away from all selfish aims, seeking truth, knowledge and wisdom not for his own purposes but in order that he may help others. He must learn to be indifferent to results, to accept apparent failure, even defeat, with equanimity. He must be willing to detach himself from the activities of the group mind and the group aims of his fellow men who still in the main function collectively; but at the same time he must never be indifferent to their needs nor detached from an attitude of deep sympathy with their problems and their sufferings. He must stand always with boldness upon his chosen path, ready to act fearlessly as he deems right and if that action be mistaken to learn from it and pay the price demanded, seeking to turn the result somehow into good. He must be prepared to give years to this strenuous training as would an athlete who trains for the course. He must have patience infinite nor seek to arouse before their time those faculties which lie dormant in every man but cannot safely be stirred into action until he be strong enough to control and direct them rightly and accept the responsibility which their awakening always entails. So having stilled the emotions, transmuted desire and ambition, he will begin to function upon that plane where truth may be apprehended, the plane of intuition whereon the Soul can touch its divine Source.

"But above all he must realize that it is through this alignment with his Soul, and only through this, that the fulfilment of these conditions becomes possible. Thus his main task will be to perfect this alignment, building the rainbow bridge between his lower consciousness and his higher Principles, so that there may be created a shining pathway down which soul wisdom may pour into its vehicle of matter on earth, which vehicle—the personality the man knows as himself—was created for that ultimate purpose and for that alone.

"Only when this bridge is built and the man's soul can act freely as a link between the personality and the true God Within will he be ready to serve devas and men.

"Then to him will the spirits of the Fire, the Air, the Water and the Earth open wide the doors of their Kingdoms. They will unite their powers with his and through him will answer the cry which humanity, in its hour of need, is sounding forth."

II

THE SOLAR DEVA

I am a Ray from our Lord,
The Lord of Light.
He is the Fire Creative;
He is one with the Hidden Word
Which, thrilling through the Cosmos,
Maketh itself manifest
In the mighty Builders
Whose reflections
Am I.

I am the Intermediary;
Through me in my multitudinous forms
Pulseth for ever
The urge, which is Life.

I am the Response;
In me sounds the Note
Which calls to the Shining Ones,
The atoms of energy,
Whirling, propelling them
Into the mystic dance
Which becometh a planet, a star,
A man—or a clod of earth.

I am the Destroyer;
When the Note changeth,
Into myself,
Into the vortex of my being,
I withdraw.
Slowly the rhythm grows fainter;
The atoms disintegrate;
The impulsions pass onward

Into another womb.
One form is no more;
Another cometh to birth.

I am limitless;
For I vibrate to the pulse
Of That which hath no limitation.
I obey.
I thrill to the bliss
Of That which, in harmony,
Worketh ever towards perfection
Through my Lord, the Hidden, the mysterious SUN.
I am the focus for That
Which is nameless and unconditioned.
I expand—I contract.
I am conscious in the infinitesimal life of the earth's core;
I rejoice with the joy of the blossom opening to the light;
I am the song of the Heavenly Ones, the Note of creation;
From whatsoever plane I receive in my being
The thrill of harmony, of creative desire—of love,
To that I respond—to that call I come;
Swifter than thought I come;
Yea, at the thought I am there;
For I am that.

O Thou Effulgent Life,
Love manifested forth
Into man's darkness,
I, flame of Thy Flame,
Dwell in Thy Heart of Light.
At Thy command I speed
Blazing with triple fires
Into the hearts of those who can invoke Thy Power.
As yet only few have learnt
To gaze without flinching into Thy dread face;
And unto them,
In the deep silence of the Fire
Which burneth ever without heat

Thy voice is heard.
To these, the Enlightened Ones, is given
Power to reflect something of what they see
Into the more receptive minds among the sons of men,
That they may glimpse the shadow of Thy glory
Mercifully tempered to their weakness,
And vision faintly That of which all are a part.
'Tis we—'tis we—glad spirits, sons of the Flame, are
    used
To draw man unto Thee, his Source;
'Tis we who inspire in him love and desire
For Thee, Light of his being;
And through Thy pure essence,
Thy spiritual glory
We seek to evolve from the youth of the world
A new race to serve Thee,
Who, lit by Thy Light and inspired by Thy Breath,
May draw from Thy Being powers of mind, spirit and
    body.
This is the work for which we were created—
The evolution of form, the releasing of spirit
From bondage; the fusing of each flame with its primal
    fire,
The Spiritual Sun, the Logos, our Lord!
O Life of our Life,
O Heart of Pure Fire,
We worship Thee, we live to obey Thee
Who, in Thy wisdom stupendous
Controlleth Thy Sons,
The Lords of the Planets.
They, stretching Their hands toward Thee,
Invoking Thy wisdom, dwell in Thy light.
Thou dost direct their impulsions,
Their courses, their wills;
Preventing the conflict of their mighty forces
Which stream ever outward
Affecting each other, as man's every action
For good or for ill, affects the lives of his brothers.

Thou blendest their notes, interweaving their harmonies
Into new forms;
Renewing their life and the lives of all beings
Who are part of their substance,
Forever evolving toward that perfection,
The form archetypal,
Revealed unto Thee through divine Ideation.
For behold, even Thou, Solar Logos, our Lord,
Even Thou bendest Thy shining head to the will of
    Another,
Knowing Thyself but a part of a mightier Scheme,
Of which He, the Unknown One, the Centre,
Is no more than the servant of ONE great beyond thought,
WHO again stretches upward, growing, evolving
In knowledge and wisdom,
Towards THAT which is Nameless,
Which is DARKNESS and SILENCE.

．　　．　　．　　．

O man, who at last, once more
Yearns towards knowledge;
We see you—we hear you,
Struggling upward—awakening; casting off the fetters
    of custom.
Naked and strong as the Greeks, the Egyptians,
Worshippers of the Sun,
Who drew life from His rays and rejoiced in His light.
Raise up your hearts again to the Lord of your being!
For growth, healing, enlightenment send forth supplica-
    tion!
Prepare to receive the powers which He bringeth
Unto His votaries:
The strong form perfected—temple fitted for light;
The mind clear and lucid;
And greatest of all, the spirit untrammelled
That leapeth to heights divine,
That uniteth itself with the rays of the planets,
That defieth destruction;

That entereth fearless
Within the dread Portals,
Into the Primal Fire,
Into the One Life,
Into the Heart of the Sun.

III

THE EARTH SPIRIT

A strange vibration pulses through my being;
I am aware of one working upon my rays
Who, through power and through devotion
Unites himself with the creative impulse
Which makes me what I am.
Now I direct my sight upon him;
I see the bright colours of his ringing Note,
Hear the pure rose and gold sounding within his heart,
Sweet strains of music which unite him
Unto us, whose focus is the growth and death
Of all things in the Second[1] Kingdom.
We approach him, I and my servants,
Nature sprites and gnomes,
Bright flower fairies and the dancing undines
That haunt the brooks,
All elementals that do work in earth, in water, sun or air.
Unto such men as this, our friend and our co-worker,
One with me and mine, Nature unveils her face.
At his vibration, strong, harmonious with her will,
Life stirs with eagerness in flower and plant.
To him we reveal our secret lore.
Love is the link between us,
For love is the primal impulse throughout the whole
    creation:
Desire for growth and union
With That which is greater than the separate self,
The mighty Being of which we and they
And all that dwell on earth are cells of life:
The Planetary Logos,
He is our life; we draw our life from Him.
Feeding upon His substance for our growth

[1] The vegetable Kingdom.

49

We each become a mystic centre wherein His will can
　　manifest
And His mysterious purpose work
From highest unto lowest.
O, far into the earth my forces flow!
The metals, the rocks, stir in their motionless and dream-
　　like state
As, uniting my consciousness with their indwelling life,
I re-charge their chemical atoms, separating the ele-
　　ments I need,
Drawing into myself a million tiny beings to work my
　　will,
And within the unseen vortices of earth,
Stimulate growth where death seems lord of life.
I cause the water devas of the air to build their cloudy
　　edifices,
And pour down their rain on thirsting fields.
'Tis I who call upon the sons of fire to send their vitalizing
　　rays
That they may fecundate the waiting earth.
Within my being, the lesser ones, my children,
Leap and play in mystic dance like motes in sunlight,
　　dazzling through the air;
Winged by the impulse of my will they fly to their
　　appointed tasks.
All things in nature play their little part within the vaster
　　plan.
The unseen insects creeping through the grass;
The honey bee winging his heavy way through clover
　　fields;
The singing bird, building his tiny nest;
The flowers, the plants, the trees—
Which love and live more consciously than all the other
　　brethren of their kind—
Each builds and lives and dies according to the Law.
Guided by One mind, our lesser minds unite;
Changing our forms, unceasingly we work in blissful
　　ecstasy.

That which seems death to you, O man,
To us is perfect rhythm, a harmony of millions of voices
Sweeping throughout the spheres in outpourings of
    joy.
Nowhere is there cessation of that song called Life.
All life createth life.
The great wheels turn in cyclic motion
Bearing all things toward one consummation.
But the one discord is the voice of man
Who, in his ignorance, still strives to work apart.
Ah, if he knew his power! If he but understood
How, because of him, the harmony remaineth in-
    complete,
For he only can retard the upward surge of evolution!
Yet already in the dim recesses of his perturbèd mind,
Like a small seed within which the life force striveth
Through its dark prison of earth toward the light,
The spirit urgeth him to seek release,
Driving him relentlessly ever toward the quest for Truth.
Yea, I perceive even now his Note vibrating into my
    centres
With a cry for union, for an expression of life,
Which only we can give.
Let it but grow stronger until I and mine
Are enabled to respond in joyous rapture;
Then unto his dazzled sight will be revealed
The hidden beauties of the Second Kingdom.
He shall perceive us at our work in valley, wood and
    stream;
Great shapes will fill his sky; he will commune with every
    flower,
Aye, with each stone; he will hear the transcendent
    music of the stars;
The sweeping winds, the glittering waters will reveal their
    souls and speak with him;
To him will come the birds—all the wild things, savage
    and shy alike
Will seek him out and walk beside him unafraid.

Then will he be taught to blend his energies with ours
 and work with us;
Then will he realize all Kingdoms are his own
When he hath learnt to sound their Note aright,
Give forth the Words of Power:
Love—Service—
Unity of Purpose
With That which
We serve.

IV

THE BUILDER OF FORM

A call resounds. Clear as a silver bell
It vibrates throughout the spheres
In quivering waves of light.
The Karmic hour, inevitable, strikes.
The impulse to create, stirs, strives, attracts.
From out the Holy Place,
The Secret Place
Where dwell the inner Powers which bring forth justice
    to each living thing,
Without Whose sanction nought may come to birth,
Sanction is given.
At the Word,
Magnetic waves surge forth to their appointed task.
We come—Builders of Form, we come!
Thought hath compelled us.
To that place we speed whence like hath called to like.
Invoke us and we stand ready to do thy will;
We cannot fail to answer to the Note which bids us serve.

    .   .   .   .

Behold me, I am here!
I am the matrix.
Within my mind the imaged thought shines clear;
Through me its life must come.
Whatever be the dream that glows in the creator's mind
That will I seek to build
So long as the clear thought reflects itself in me, unwaver-
    ing and unchanged.
Through every channel the great power which I may
    use
Flows in.
So much—no more.

Be it a child, a flood of music, an empire or a song that is
    conceived on earth,
The Law remains: so much force and no more.
So much! I feel the waves
Pulsing and playing in my golden heart.
A myriad lives are drawn into my life;
Mine is their joy.
Within my womb they build, they coalesce.
Potent with their new life I too expand.
I sweep their forces into patterns, shapes of colour and of
    sound.
The clear form grows.
Power is converging now with ever increasing might
Towards its focus on the physical plane.
The centres rotate in unison;
The vortex glows.

.   .   .   .

Into the heart of him whose strong desire
Conjured me forth with all the powers I wield,
The energies, the fiery atoms drive
Until the work is done.
The artist, the musician, he who seeks to trap a dream
    with words,
Actors, inventors, all those in whom the creative impulse
    stirs,
Although their minds are ignorant of me
Recognize and acclaim me when my emanations flow
    into their hearts.
Their blood runs swifter; joy leaps within their breast.
They are themselves, yet mightier than themselves
For they are also what I am.
Magnified, transfigured, glorified, they become in the
    divine moment of creative energy
One with all lives in me, and with that greater Life
Of which I am th' embodiment.
In me It manifests to them and inspiration pours into the
    mould of form.
I am the spirit of rebirth.

Through me the germs of life are coalesced
Within the mother's womb
When the configurations of the stars propitious stand.
Through my life pass the elements of this new life;
The astral currents bring to me forms from the past,
Results of causes which, generated by acts in other lives,
Until their Note sounds, sleep as if forgot.
A thousand elements co-operate.
The child's egoic self watches and aids through me,
Already tied to its inevitable fate
By thread as fine as silver spiders' web, yet strong as steel.
We draw the force from those we may.
From parents take etheric matter; from all nature's
      kingdoms, particles of life,
Little or much according to the merits of the soul which
      seeks new birth.
And as the work goes on,
Within the hidden matrix of my heart glows the child's
      form—a jewel, a bud of light.

I am the Virgin Mother; the spirit of the primaeval
      ocean
Whence all things were conceived and all forms drawn
      anew.
With me the healers come, sons of violet etheric waves
Who guide and inspire the minds of those who seek to
      understand and cure
The manifold ills of men;
For ours is the task to build humanity ever anew,
Leading it on from strength to strength, towards its full
      fruition,
The apex of its glory, the mighty Race to be, who con-
      sciously
Will see us, know us, work as now we work
In harmony with greater than we, high guardians of the
      Race, Servants of the Creative Power of Love.
Which urges all manifested life towards perfected
      harmony.

O you, the wise, co-operate with me!
Pour forth your love, your pure desire to us,
And we will quicken it and vitalize
With fire and water, with the elements of air and earth,
The Sacred Four:
Pure fire, spiritual flame, essence of life;
Water, the symbol of the astral powers, illusory, the
    fount of men's desires,
Already in all lower forms fatally intermingling.
Air, the swift, rushing messengers who come as winds to
    purify the form;
And earth, the only part man knows as yet, which binds
    him still a helpless prisoner.

Behold me then—the Messenger, glowing with love!
Evoke me—I reply.
Yet be thou warned, O man, who in thy pride and
    strength,
Thinketh perchance to use powers and elements thou
    canst not yet control.
I am the agent of the law.
To him who doth seek my rich gifts for dark forbidden
    purpose,
And would through their use create distorted shapes and
    crude disharmonies.
Evil that will curse the lives of men,
My powers indeed will come, since he hath freewill to
    choose,
But with them comes also his just retribution, for they
    will be his doom.
'Twere better he had been born as his fellow men,
Blind, deaf and dumb to these great potencies which lie
    within man's jurisdiction.
For he who useth Force against the Law
By Force will be destroyed.
But those who will learn, who even now are learning,
    how to speak
Our language, how to hear our all pervasive harmonies,

To work with us, and with us strive to obey the Will
    Divine,
Them shall the Devas gladly serve.
They shall become as we;
To them shall Truth unveil her face;
They shall be free
To wield our powers,
And sound the Note of Form.

V

THE DEVAS OF CEREMONIAL

We watch, we wait.
From man's primaeval, blind desire for union with That
    from which he came
Were we created.
We will remain with him till that desire is consummated,
And we, with man, return into the glory whence all
    things emerged.

There is no place, however low and humble, consecrated
    by the use of prayer and praise
Unblessed by one of our great Brotherhood,
And by those mightier Ones, radiant in love, who are
    our Lords.
Our strength, our beauty and our power to bless
Grow by the force which emanates from priest and
    worshipper;
According to its measure we are enabled thus
To shower our benedictions forth.
When instrument and voice unite in praise and love and
    worship,
And lifted on wings of pure one-pointed will flood us with
    power and glory,
Then we expand and glow.
Bright rays leap from our eyes; the jewel heart within
    focusseth light,
The mystic Rose unfolds.
The Word goes forth; flashing from East and West
Our Brethren come to join their strength with ours
And far and wide peace and rejoicing bless the hearts of
    men.
Magic our nature is; magic of ritual, music and word
    conjured us once

To stimulate and influence the minds of those
Who held the secret and could sound the Note
Of sacred invocation.
But now no more the mystic harmonies of sound rever-
berate through the triple worlds.
Now no more pure waves of light, fair colours, elemental
shapes
Of beauty rise from temple and from grove.
That age is past.
Now the mumbling priest, the scanty worshippers
Who cling to old traditions and whose minds like wanton
breezes
Cannot retain a thought beyond the moment;
The sad, discordant jingle of faint sound, the words,
devoid of knowledge as of sense,
Have not the power to call our glory down.
Faintly our forms appear; dimmed are our pristine rays
As shadows seen in some cracked, ancient glass.
How can we then still generate the powers which stir the
heart,
And raise man's consciousness to states of ecstasy,
Whence wisdom falls like dew upon his arid mind, and he
beholds
His Lord and ours—supreme?
Man hath forgot and turned himself away,
For those who were once the guardians of the Sacred
Lore
Have failed him and poisoned the bright wells at which
he drank;
So through the growing faculties of his awakening mind
He hath outstripped them.
No longer will he walk the mystic path whereon he thinks
that he has been deceived;
No longer doth he hope to find the truth he seeks through
ceremonial rites.
Those ancient sacraments of unsurpassèd beauty,
The united voice and act of worshippers, the rhythmic
movement,

This magic which called us to unite our consciousness
    with that of the participants,
And give them super-terrestrial vision.
This hath now become a legend—an idle poet's dream;
For from the heart of ceremonial the holy mysteries have
    been withdrawn,
And now being empty can no more answer man's need,
    for now it fails to stir his senses
Or stimulate his mind, tuned to another key.
O man, knowing no other source at which to slake your
    raging thirst for Truth,
Ye wander down strange ways, seeking your gods on
    earth,
And finding nought but broken images!
Yet ye have willed to walk alone,
And lonely, stumble through th' encompassing dark,
Unlit by those clear stars which once gave life to all your
    works.
So shall it be while still ye refuse to pass
The dread portals of the ancient Mysteries.
Now your idle feet sound hollowly on temple floors
    deserted
Where in ancient days the power of God took form
And priest initiates wrought what would to you seem
    miracles.
So ignorant have ye become, ye can no more distinguish
    error from truth;
Forfeited are your powers—and it is well.
Not yet are ye ripe for the new dawn of knowledge;
Ye have too much to learn.
Now we can give you nought but guardianship and
    pity;
We can only meet the less with less.
Nothing can come from nothing.
When once again man learns his innate need
And cries to be shown the way of wisdom,
When he seeks to unite himself with us
Through service, devotion and the rites of love,

When from the earth's aura are effused the rays of roseate
    harmony,
Where now the scarlet blaze of conflict glows,
Then to man's call the Great Ones will reply;
Then will descend on earth an impulse new;
Wise teachers will return to guide the Race and to unveil
Another aspect of the face of Truth,
Founding great schools where mysteries will be revealed
And Nature's powers disclosed to those
Who can be brave, pure, silent and controlled.
Then to meet the new needs will be evolved new forms
    of worship;
New words of Power to take the place of those
Which have been desecrated in usage base by the de-
    luded men
Who work against the Law.
When once again the celestial waves of sound rise up to
    us from earth,
Calling us down in glory and in might,
Then in that day we shall descend with power,
Our pure Ray shining forth anew in all its pristine
    beauty,
In symphonies of colour, light and sound.
Then, heralded by us, will return in majesty,
The mighty Lord of Love,
Who cometh only when through love and ardent desire
    for growth,
Man calleth Him down into the place prepared where
    He can manifest.
In your own hands, O man, is your own fate.
Time for us is not.
Until that day dawn when, strong and wise,
Ye understand yourselves and use aright your own
    glorious potentialities,
We, your servants, brothers, lords,
We watch—we wait.

VI

THE NATIONAL DEVA

I am the great Guardian;
I unite and coalesce within my being the hopes and
  aspirations
Generated by that chosen group of men I live to
  serve.
I am the embodiment of the national thought,
The people's tendencies, their dreams, their aspirations,
The invisible symbol of their collective life,
The Form they have themselves, through their own
  highest thoughts, evolved.
I stand perpetually brooding o'er their land;
I change with their continual changing;
I evolve with them.
To me is given power to mitigate through transmutation
Their errors, in accordance with the will for good in-
  herent in them.
I am their pride of Race.
I come to birth at the first national act,
And from that moment evermore I work upon their
  hidden centres,
Leading them on and upward.
At the beginning, when, like a tender child
The Nation stumbles, with small control, unity of will
  and purpose,
I focus its aspirations in mine own clear heart, stimulating
  its self-consciousness,
Filling it with desire for achievement and to shine above
  its fellows;
I segregate it, turning it inward upon itself;
Feed it with religions proper to its spiritual growth;
I give it lines of kings, that it may learn to idealize itself
  in them;

I give it lords of war and peace, leaders and teachers to
   intensify
Its energies within the triple worlds of matter, mind and
   spirit.
Thus I do lead its childish steps towards maturity.
Later when it hath grown and the urge for expansion,
   prowess and adventure stirs within,
Then do I fire the imaginations of its poets with a thou-
   sand chimeras of glory,
And lead the Nation forth to where its capacities
May find expression and a wider scope.
Then it doth break its childhood bonds; it sendeth its
   sons
To gather ideas, innovations, material benefits from
   others of its kind;
To bear it children in far foreign lands, to conquer it
   fields
Where it may sow its seed, expand and grow.
Thus cometh it to its prime.
At last, flushed with achievement, proud, remote, apart,
It toucheth the danger line.
Strong, self-centred, in this its glorious maturity
It wills to stand supreme,
And draws into itself currents from every source, both
   good and ill.
It inciteth envy and fear.
Now it may become dazzled by desire for domination,
Enslaved by those vain ambitions which are conceived
   through pride;
Men rise within its heart, inspired by the Dark Forces
   who
Seek ever to bring confusion to the earth.
They urge the Nation forth on paths of useless conquest;
They drive it to desire powers that it cannot hold and far
   less can control,
Stimulating all evil tendencies which it hath generated
   throughout its past.
Now is its hour of choice—its testing time.

For in it now, as in the body of man when once the apex
 of his life is passed,
The strength of youth is over, and the downward arc of
 form, of matter, hath begun,
Disintegrations stirs.
Three pathways lie before it:
It may remain static, and tainted by inertia fall into quick
 decay;
Or through pride and vain excess, through evil counsel,
 and a refusal
To see the truth, blindly it may rush on toward its
 inevitable doom,
Defeat, eclipse, annihilation.
But it can take the noblest path of all
And, turning once more its forces inward
Toward the things of mind and spirit, seek to perfect that
 work for which it was conceived.
Then let it listen to the voice of those wise guardians of
 the Race,
The great men of its past, who bound to it by service and
 by love
Have become its Guides, its Teachers and who, unknown,
 still serve it from their secret hiding-places.
Let it lay its bright sword aside, and strive with Them for
 peace.
Inspired by Them evolve its fiery potencies—the fruits
 of its endeavour on the long path of evolution—
Toward still greater heights of spiritual achievement and
 of glory
Before its day be done.
For pass it must; the circle of birth and death is to be
 trod by all,
Man, Nation, World and System—that is the Law.
But O, my child, my offspring and creater both,
Be wise, refuse annihilation and the scorn which is given
 to the weak and fallen;
Make thy decline a glory!
Let the powers of spirit and of mind exalt it,

Let thine eyes shine with the light of youth eternal;
Unite thy hidden fires with those immortal Fires which
　　burn in the mighty Beings,
Who brood over continents and oceans, who guide the
　　policies of every race.
O, send me forth through the impulsion of thy enlight-
　　ened understanding
To unite myself with Them, The International Devas,
Who, to the world, are what I am to thee.
Then through their regenerating power new energy will
　　re-vitalize.
Thy dying form.
Thou wilt blaze up, thou wilt become a guiding star to
　　Nations younger than thyself;
A torch by which men yet unborn shall see the Path to
　　wisdom.
Then through the impulse that thy transcendent power
　　will give to life and form,
The greater world outside thyself will grow; taking its
　　ideals of leadership.
From thy renowned example.
Races to come will pour their blessing on thy name,
And thou wilt live again in them, through them receive
The transcendent gift of Immortality.

VII

THE INTERNATIONAL DEVA

We are the mighty Brotherhood of Peace and Evolution,
Ensoulèd first through the great mind of Him
The Planetary Lord,
Himself the reflection of a higher Will,
He, our Father, who stands guardian
Over his children, great and small alike,
Protecting them in love from those great cosmic forces
Which, if allowed to enter his domain unchecked,
Would sweep all to destruction.
Watchful we dwell above man's surging tides of con-
     flict,
Discerning the activities of earth as currents
Of colour and sound, filaments of energy
We seek to draw together, interweave
Into the sacred pattern we have been shown
By Him who guides us all.
We strive ever for unity.
Our task is to harmonize those discordant notes
Which every separate nation emanates
Swelling the cacophonous voice of this sad world.
We work through our lesser Brethren who, nearer to
     man,
Sensitive to his thought and aims, reveal to us
The trend of his development.
Acting as intermediaries, drawing to those
Ready to respond, the energies they need
From out our heart of wisdom;
Seeking to lead man to enlightenment
That he may glimpse the pattern of the Plan
Join in our work for peace, further our aims.
We it is who magnetize those centres
Where leaders of men gather to plan

Methods of international co-operation, to seek out paths
of peace,
And to inaugurate reforms and laws to benefit mankind.
From the regenerating flame of their desire, we strive to
create the harmony necessary to their ends.
'Tis we who inspire the minds of their great men—bright
lights shining through chaos—
Who, in response to our divine vibrations, invoke,
through visions of progress, our power.
We endeavour to transmute the errors and the fears, the
conflicts and confusions
Which arise through man's own blindness, into ultimate
benefit, bringing swift retribution
That he may learn to associate Cause and Effect and
recognize that evil and destruction breed nought
but dissolution,
And love and harmony alone will lead him toward the
perfect State
Of which his leaders and his seers dream.
Thus do we ever seek to draw all men into our own
Brotherhood
Revealing to them the foolishness of separation and racial
prejudice,
Necessary to the young but fatal curse on older nations
who must learn to live in bonds of harmony or
perish.
'Tis we, who, at this time, are striving to unite the spiritual wisdom of the East to those fine qualities of
lower mind.
The West hath now developed.
For until East and West can comprehend each others'
thought,
Until the barriers of race and creed are down, and all
men know that Truth is one;
Until each country hath passed through the hot fires of
experience and mastered its own control,
Finding its unity within and realizing that each one is
part of all;

Until that time peace cannot reign on earth.

For discord lies, like to a snake, hidden within the tangled
growth of separateness.

We are all One. Ye Nations of the earth ye are the
limbs, the organic forces, the dense body

Of the Planetary Lord.

Whilst ye remain in this fell state of discord and war
perpetually the one against the other,

Ye set up spiritual diseases, cancers, poisons, within the
body of Him, your great Father,

Who, incorporating mankind, hath sacrificed Himself

To raise you to His own transcendent height,

And so by you He serves is held from further progress.

For know that all things, even the mightiest Beings
advance inevitably toward some higher goal,

Striving towards perfection.

From atom to god, the Law repeats itself in ever widening
circles.

Through harmony alone can Nations grow; through arts
and sciences, through music, through spiritual
vision;

Those higher potencies in man which rise ever superior
to the illusory barriers of race or creed or speech,

As the pure mountain heights serenely stand above the
confusions of the valley's life.

Only through fuller comprehension and acceptance of
these immutable laws

Can race combine with race. For these laws are our very
essence;

They are the majestic rhythm of the Thought divine;
bright gleams from that ineffable Source which
flows toward at-one-ment.

Through us, who work as one, its harmonies, the primordial Songs of the creative Sons of Love,

Are ever poured into the minds of those who can contact
us.

O man, strive then to rend the veil which hides us
still;

Aspire towards perfection, unity of purpose and of
    thought!
Then will all men, all nations, every Race, sounding out
    each his own perfected chord,
Unite in one transcendent symphony.
And we shall blaze forth in glory blending our Note with
    yours,
Bringing you bliss and love supernal, drawing you up-
    ward on mighty chords of sound,
Higher and higher, till the Apex reached,
Perfected man unites with his Great Self
And passes beyond the bounds of Earth
To another Scheme
And to another Dawn.

VIII

THE DIVINE MUSICIAN

I am the harbinger of Love and Peace,
The embodiment of Music,
The perfected symphony of fair thoughts and deeds
    blending in unison.
All life is set to music.
By music do the stars spiral together through their courses;
The interplay of every force, from whirl of smallest atom
To that of the Thought issuing forth from out the Night
    of Chaos—
The Song of Vishnu which gives birth to a new Creative
    Day
And rouses the Sons of Action from inertia—
Sound forth a sacred mantram,
Divine chromatics man cannot hear as yet, although he,
    day and night
Giveth himself forth sound, evil or good, discordant or
    euphonious
According to his nature.
It is from these unceasing tones and overtones
Rising from man's own heart,
Disjunctive waves of broken melody,
Flashes of pure beauty, angry orchestrations of fiendish
    dissonance,
That I, the messenger between man and those great
    Ones
Who brood over his destiny, seek ever to blend,
And to transmute through my pure heart of love.
I am a ray from that divine Musician
Who wrought with sound the mystic Word of Power
In that creative dawn when Life emerged from Chaos.
I am the harbinger
Of that celestial music of the spheres

Which those, sensitive to our voices, catch
In faint, elusive echoes, weaving it
Into great works of glory which will touch
The yearning hearts of men with ecstasy
Responsive to a magic that can give
Release to earth's pains and burdens.
When men gather together to perform the great creative
    works
Wherewith we inspire the mighty sons of music on the
    earth,
There in the air above we surge in serried ranks
Building amid the scintillating colours which notes and
    chords give forth
Shapes of transcendent beauty,
Into the heart of which, upon the wings of sound, we raise
All those who listen to sublimest heights of rapture;
And, using this mighty power, radiate love and unity
Upon all the world around.
What once the Priesthood did, that now we do through
    music;
We are the hierophants of the Mysteries,
Seeking to raise through sound man's wandering heart
    to God.
In all the forms which love creates
My attributes are mirrored.
In the clear effulgence which is given forth
By the desire to cherish and protect the weak, the ailing
    and pitiful,
Whose light is dim or turgid and whose minds whirl in
    discordant cadences of pain;
In the quiet harmony of peaceful homes;
In the manifestations of the powers of sex through love
That symbol of the universal urge which seeks,
Balancing the pairs of opposites,
In every form, from Planetary Lord to smallest atom,
To blend and merge
The aspects twain into one Perfection—
I manifest my powers of synthesis.

In mother-love—that glowing shaft of rose, that thrill of
    melody;
In any selfless joy; in children's laughter;
In every aspect of the love divine which man,
As yet unwittingly, creates ever anew
Within his heart's bright centre, there I work.
I am a part of all quiet, secret joys.
The sweet singing of the small wild bird;
The voice of patient beasts rising from dim fields at
    eventide;
The sibilant whisper of the sun-kissed grass;
The chime of bells across the evening air;
The song of wind and water
All notes in Nature's chant of ecstasy
Which, blending, form a mighty orchestra
Yet are but one chord in the celestial song
Rising from every star and planet, every universe
Thrilling ever throughout the Cosmos.
From man alone comes discord;
He alone is deaf to the transcendant harmony of the
    Spheres.
Yet by my art I seek to integrate
His harsh, destructive sounds
Through blending them with sweeter melodies
From a miriad loving hearts,
Pouring these down again in blessing
On whosoever can respond to them.
Seek then to give, that giving, ye may receive
Ye men, who now toil blindly, weep and strive in conflict;
Open your hearts in love, vibrate to my pure ray,
Hark to its emanations.
Then shall ye draw from me such wealth of peace and
    beauty
That ye, o'er filled with bliss, will radiate perforce
Its surplus out into that vast reservoir,
The vortex of healing regenerating power, wherein all
    energy is garnered.
By Those whom I serve, the men divine

Who once were like to you, but now
Stand on the mountain heights
Seeking to draw their brethren to that fount
Of joy to which they have through many weary lives at
    last attained.
They are your Masters; and it is through them,
Adepts indeed of love,
That perfect harmony is wrought.
It is to them we, luminous spirits, bring these streams of
    sound
This living power which riseth ever from mankind to
    God,
For them to use according to man's need,
Returning the regenerated force again through us, upon
    the earth;
Sounding great chords which rise, expand, outflow
In forms of power which send an ecstatic thrill through
    all your world.
Thus, O man, what ye in ignorance have given
That, through the Law of Love, ye receive once more,
    but glorified beyond knowledge.
For whatso'er ye give of good or ill,
Inevitably that will return to you.
In this lies your power, your glory—and your woe.
Listen and hear the Law,
The Law which They, your forerunners, obeyed:
He who dare make the sacrifice for Love,
He who, through Love has suffered and been consumed,
Through Love shall be reborn, and in Love find the
    uttermost completion.
Within him shall then be generated the most glorious
    powers
Which only those who sound forth the Note of Unity
Have earned the right to claim:
To bring joy unto the sorrowful;
Hope to those who dwell in the house of weeping;
To bring light to the blind, to open the ears of those who
    are deaf

To the secret melodies of the spheres divine;
To heal those who are sick;
To bring strength to the weak, peace to the afflicted, life
    from the tomb.
Yea, he who could learn to use the mystic Words aright,
To sound the keynote of each living thing,
He would be lord of devas and of men,
Building, disintegrating at his will.
But few there are yet who have unveiled the secret;
Close still it lies hid behind adamantine doors.
First must man learn to rule himself,
To sound his own personal note aright,
In harmony with other men and with the Cosmic note
    of Love.
Through training, self-discipline and unremitting service
He cometh to that Door which leads to the Temple
    Courts.
Upon the Door are writ the words: "Love. Serve. Obey.
    Be Silent."
Thence doth the path wind up, toilsome and long.
Yet only to him who follows this path alone
Will be disclosed powers transcendental.
And when at last the greater part of living men
Can wield the secrets and can sound the Notes,
Then man shall hear and see
The supernal rhythms of the creative song;
Then shall we at long last with him unite
Our powers, working with him in joyous harmony.
Then shall the earth, redeemed at length
Sound forth her own sweet note, unsullied, pure,
With those, her Brethren, who hymn their bright paths
In consort throughout the universe.
Then shall man know at last that he is one
With All; one with the accomplished harmony of God.

IX

THE SPIRIT OF LIGHTNING

He who can learn to cup my power within the little
    chalice of his mind,
He who can transmute my elements, my warring attri-
    butes, through his own heart's centre,
Discerning in them th' eternal harmonies of those great
    Cosmic forces
Which oft to men appear destructive,
On him my gifts descend.
Through him my fire shall flow in vitalizing streams,
Into those whirling centres, the Holy Seven,
Wherein are generated his own internal life fires,
Most sacred flames, giving, to him alone who stands
    prepared,
The Powers to make of man a god;
Powers which are mocked at still by those
Who vainly seek to unfold the mysteries of the hidden
    lore
But to abuse them for their own base ends;
So little fitted is man still for knowledge.
Indeed they know me not; nor will they know me yet.
They peer into the dark, blinded by the limitations they,
    in their senseless pride,
Have imposed upon themselves.
But I am there—within them and without.
For I am Child of Agni, mysterious creative Fire
Secret and sacred beyond man's understanding.
I am the furnace which burns out all dross;
Leaving pure gold;
I am the glow-worm's light;
I am the incandescent heat
Which blazes from the heart of greater suns
Than man shall ever find, for all his skills

The faintest gleam from which would burn his brain
Into dull ash.
Yet am I too the heat he useth, easing his life,
Serving his daily needs most humbly.
I am those sparks unseen
Which animate his being.
I am each aspect of the all-pervasive Flame.
I am the Fire which strikes, destroys, disintegrates,
Purifying the festering plague spots of the earth,
Those centres where, through foolishness of man,
In pestilential streams evil wells up,
With wild, discordant sounds and vaporous loathly
    forms, colours of hell,
Which, when they reach a certain potency—generating
    a force that might, unchecked
Pollute the creative rays ever poured down
To fecundate the earth and raise men's hearts to con-
    cord—
Must be destroyed by us, as once Atlantis was,
Through fires, floods and cataclysms.
I am the regenerator.
When intertia falleth, like a blight
Upon mankind, and men grow fat, complacent, during
    some phase
Of material prosperity—good Karma earned in the past
By those who have not yet grown wise enough
To know how best to utilize the good to benefit man-
    kind—
Then do I come like to a cloud of hornets on a summer
    day
And sting man to activity again,
So that, his body roused from out its slothful ease, his
    mind alert,
He rises up to face his destiny.
Self preservation is the goad which hath from man's
    forgotten past
Pricked him along the thorny path of evolution,
And 'tis this chord I strike in every key, in every octave,

Until at last I sound it, ringing, upon the highest note
Where man seeketh no more to preserve against my fires
His little separate self,
But now defendeth that other self, mankind,
The body of his Lord, Regent of Earth.
Yea, he who desireth nothing for himself, who dares
    unite with me his higher mind,
And brave my lightning and my Note which shatters
    him
Whose motive is impure,
To him shall I disclose the secrets of my Power.
In him shall the Serpent raise its fiery head;
The bright wheels shall revolve and he shall see
The atoms whirling in their destined path;
He shall begin to glimpse the pattern and the immensity
    of the Cosmic Plan.
He shall hear an echo of the stupendous harmonies
Through which eternally manifests the Law.
He shall become that Law, the purging fire—
For I am That.
Then, fused in my lambent heart, he will perceive clear-
    eyed
How we, the mighty agents of the Law, strike.
Then shall he know that justice rules, and knowing shall
    feel
Surging within him the same fierce joy that surges
    through our being,
At the commands of God.
Then, working in harmony with us, he will unite his
    little force
With that stupendous force of which he is a part.
Then shall his small flame leap up, and glow and burn,
Merging once more into that primordial fire which is
    himself and all things.
But he who fears us; he who hath not yet learned
The hidden secrets of our hierarchy,
The union of will with that great purpose which is our
    God;

Or he who hath abused the majesty of Fire,
Let him not seek me out.
He shall be shattered; him will mine eyes blind.
Beneath the onslaught of my lightning, the thunders of
    my voice,
His quivering nerves and his o'er-chargèd brain shall reel
    and faint
Until he cry, without avail, for peace,
Admitting himself foolish, blind, powerless, before the
    gaze of truth.
Then, knowing, haply, he may turn again and seek
    enlightenment,
Asking to be taught the mysteries of Being,
And find at length that in my hands which slay,
And in my voice which shatters the unworthy, and in
    mine eyes
From which the lightnings strike,
Is Peace for him whose heart is one with All.

X

THE BUILDERS OF THE NEW AGE

We are the architects of the New Age,
The builders of the coming Race of men,
Inaugurators of the Cyclic change.
Through us the future speaks;
Through us its Note is sounded forth, its Form is given,
    and its Name made known . . .

Within our centres we become aware of mysteries stirring
Further than our outmost boundaries of contact;
For HE our Lord, Soul of the Sun,
Withdrawn in profoundest meditation beyond all
    bournes of knowledge
Has once again let the great Word go forth.
He and His Brethren,
The Planetary Lords
Have drawn aside another veil.
Their bright regard hath plunged into far realms of
    unrevealèd wisdom
Until this hour, unknown by any, save THOSE e'en
    mightier than They.
Now by this act have they become
Initiates in new Powers beyond all ken or thought.
And the dynamic currents from Their supernal minds,
Re-charged by this stupendous revelation,
Rush forth, stimulating every cell
Within the worlds which constitute Their bodies.
From some far secret Solar System
At the reverberations of the great Note,
Magnetic waves, new forces carrying potentialities
As yet undreamed of by humanity
Are straight released, radiating through interplanetary
    space

And Form responds upon the Seven Planes.
Those Who Know
Sound forth the Notes creative, ope wide the door
Towards the earth, their focus.
Then do we arise,
Servants of Christ,
Bearing aloft the chalice
Whence shall flow forth
The living Waters from the Source of Being.

Around us gather now vast hosts of devas
Regents of Kingdoms to which man is heir—
Wanderer in far lands, oblivious of his heritage—
Powers of Air and Fire, of Waters, builders of form
They who guide race and nation,
All who respond to the future's clarion note,
Swiftly we gather.
Who shall resist us?
Who but the dark sons of inertia
Holding mankind in thraldom to the forms
Crystallized in the thoughts of the dead past;
Who but the blind who cling still to tradition
Seek to turn time's wheel backward
Agents of darkness, resisting enlightenment.

O long will the conflict rage on the planet!
Long before those who respond to the call of the future
And those who reject it,
Merging their powers, find reconciliation
Acclaiming the Present, harbinger of hope,
Of the Christchild, the Saviour.

But now there is conflict.
The Note of the past is shattered in discords;
At the presage of change
Man feels his whole world, his security menaced;
For deep in his being he senses
Dissolution, the pitiless threat of unknown tomorrows,

Seeing not that they bear also the promise of birth
Into a future of glory and beauty.
Fearing nought but catastrophe,
Over his head the shadow of death
The threat to his world of total annihilation,
In desperate terror he clings still to the safety
Of old incantations, invoking the magic
Of an age which is passing
From which power has departed:
So painful, so slow is the death of convictions
Which once promised salvation
But have grown impotent—empty.
Cease now your struggle 'gainst the tides of the future
Cease blindly repulsing the Powers which would save
    you
O man, who inherits the promise of ages.
Those who still fail to press forward and onward
Will go down 'neath the onslaught
Of the incoming forces, the Powers of the future.
To refuse to relinquish the past is forbidden
And brings but disaster,
For that which is static must die.
But as for their brethren,
The sons of Aquarius,
Seekers for truth, who from swift feet and eager
Shake the dust of old dreams,
Who demand Light and knowledge and wisdom,
To these will I speak words of power and of glory;
To them, only to them
Will I unveil my face
Show my radiant Presence
That form archetypal, goal of man's aspirations.
Yes, you shall behold me
Standing uplifted 'twixt the earth and the heavens
On the pinions of dawn
The dawn of the New Age,
Cleaving asunder the thick mists of ignorance,
Holding up to your vision the glass wherein, mirrored,

He who dare lift his gaze shall perceive the reflection
Of the future—the glory of mankind triumphant.

O Warrior, my brother, thou who hast pledged thy-
    self
To work with our hosts for man's regeneration,
How couldst thou know me until deep in thy being
The voice of thy Lord could sound forth my Note?
Behold, now I greet thee
Accept thee as co-worker with the hosts of the devas.
Strange wilt thou find our paths,
Stranger will be our language
Yet we shall instruct thee
Lead thee and guide thee
To be our intermediary
Revealing our powers to men.
Yet be warned, O bold seeker,
Art thou willing to pass through the portals of Flame
To receive initiation into the Mysteries
Of the Age of Aquarius
And enter the hazardous realms of the Devas?
For thou wilt return a brand for the burning,
A scapegoat, the sacrifice for those who, behind thee,
Blinded by truth may rend and destroy thee.
But if thou be courageous, armed with love and com-
    passion,
If still thou desirest to work with me and my brothers,
Then lift thy mind above the confusions of the earth;
Gaze clear-eyed upon truth. Fear nothing! In struggle,
    in defeat,
Aye, even in death, is strength added to strength.
Through knowledge shall thy mind become lucid and
    stable;
Thou shalt Know and for ever be freed from all doubting.
Then will I guide thee through the caves of Emotion, the
    tides of Desire, into the fires of my being.
I will change and transmute thee, that in thy mind, as
    in those of thy fellows—

The seers, the creators—the events of the future shall be
    faintly reflected.
For know, O my child, that the time now approacheth
When in man's form among you will come for your
    guidance,
The harbingers of the New Age.
Disciples of Christ.
Ancient wrongs must be righted, the balance adjusted.
Not for man alone shineth the new dawn.
The sons of the Third[1] shall rejoice with their masters.
To them also cometh an Avatar, a redeemer.
He, Lord of the beasts, will teach man to repay
The debt that he oweth to his little brothers
Whom still he doth slay for greed or for wanton sport,
Breaking the laws divine, destroying that harmony,
    which is goal of Creation.
Herein lies the schism; this is the curse on man
Who was given, in ancient times, lordship over the
    earth, the three lower kingdoms.
For upon him the charge was laid to shield and to
    guide
All forms of that life—those forms once his own—
And lead them upward along the ascending arc of
    evolution.
That charge he doth betray with every act of suffering
    he doth cause,
E'en though, in selfish blindness, he may persuade him-
    self the act be justified;
Thus hath he brought the judgment on himself that he,
    by causing confusion in the lower worlds,
By using his great power for basest ends, cannot himself
    find peace
Until he hath repaid these ancient debts.
The New Race will be shown by Him who cometh the
    path of regeneration.
And, quickened by these new waves of planetary force
    which even now

[1] Animal Kingdom.

Are playing upon the earth, man will evolve the powers
      to perceive
The inner truth, to read the souls of plants, animals and
      men,
To enter, through the magic of sympathy and love, all
      kingdoms
Higher and lower than his own.
Devas will be his teachers. His eye of light shall be
      unclosed
And he will see then into fair realms he now derideth.
Then shall he be taught the powers of speech. He shall
      address
Devas and gods in their own language.
His kings and statesmen then will be Initiates
And will contact the great Ones for guidance in the
      affairs of man.
Thus will the race, through centuries of striving, rise
      toward a still more glorious stage;
Illumination will pour once more from on high.
In that far day the more advanced of that Sixth Race of
      men,
Will have transmuted sex, conquered emotion and
      transmuted transitory desire;
This high aim accomplished, then will they be taught
To use the powers of mind to build the bodies of their
      children;
And to combine in these most glorious beings, the finer
      qualities of either sex:
Purified love, intuition, powerful, one-pointed will,
Wisdom, activity—the secrets of creation, so that they in
      their turn, may build in sound, colour and form.
Long must ye wait for this.
Yet even now, for him who hath eyes to see, the first faint
      signs
Of this far, promised day are manifest, for already
The beneficent gods draw mankind towards their goal.
Into the minds of those whose imaginations, winged by
      burning desire

To help the world are uplifted for one ecstatic instant into
    the realm of Ideation
Where time is not and the goal can be perceived.
Transient flashes from this bright dawn appear.
Into their hands is given the torch lit by this flame divine,
    this rising sun of glory.
It is for them, whom I have sealed to be my messengers,
To guide man's faltering steps toward this light.
It is for them, forerunners of the new age, whose eyes
    have looked into mine own,
Whose ears have heard my voice, to launch their breth-
    ren forth upon the great, surging tides of evolu-
    tion;
To be their pilot and their guiding star, drawing them
    ever upward towards the sacred heights,
The Holy Mountain, birth-place of the Race to be,
Where Man, his eyes opened, shall at last behold himself
Transfigured, glorified,
Himself no more
But merged and one with All.

XI

THE GUARDIAN OF THE HEIGHTS

I am the Spirit of the Mountains,
The symbolic form of life in every stage.
From the dull earth—the body—I arise
To water, restless and illusory like man's desires;
Thence my seams soar upward to those pure heights serene
Where nought stirs but the great wind of Spirit
Sweeping over icy snows; where the rays from our Lord
    the Sun
Pour down unchecked by atmospheric veils.
I am the sacred Mount,
The unfolding Lotus;
The dense body of that Holy One,
Soul of the Earth—the Silent Watcher.
In me are combined all elements and kingdoms;
In me all potentialities unite from lowest to highest.
My feet are set deep in the Central Fires;
Deep in the secret place where the great Snake is curled,
Where gaseous elements unite to transmute the eternally
    whirling atoms,
Where stability taketh its final dense, illusory form.
Here spirit burns and crystallizes into the treasures of the
    mineral world:
Rubies and emeralds; diamonds, the emblem of Will and
    Knowledge;
And gold that hath the power to set men's passions
    flaming with greed.
Molten processes, chemical changes that the scientists—
    e'en alchemists of old—
Imagined not, are here created by infinite, swarming
    forms of life:
Gnomes, salamanders, dark elemental shapes, mindless
    instinctive beings,

Etheric giants and pigmies, who know not light of sun,
  or breath of air.
Tremendous forces stir in my dark depths, servants of the
  great Law.
Sometimes, propelled by mysterious cosmic changes, or
  invoked,
By mankind's own destructive emanations,
The Terrible Ones, who dwell within the vortices of
  earth's profoundest caverns
Are roused from their dread sleep, and rending their
  prison house
Arise with glaring eyes and pinions dark into the upper
  air.
Then the rocks crack, th' internal fires belch forth;
All life within the bounds of their jurisdiction is straight
  extinguished,
Continents are sunk and oceans churn.
The spirits of the blue magnetic fires, the Great Regener-
  ators,
Shiva's mighty sons, leap to the call.
Destroyers and creators both, they cleanse the planet,
  building it anew
With fresh combinings of our elements to serve its
  needs.
We are the bony structure of the world, its mighty back-
  bone, nerves and arteries
Through which the sacred forces flow which give it life
  and health
And feed the myriad beings who take from it their
  substance.
We it is, the tall mountain gods, who draw from all our
  planes
The living forces up to that high peak where air and
  ether meet,
Transmuting them into spiritual qualities in higher
  spheres beyond the ken of man.
From out our secret centres well the springs, life-blood
  of the earth,

To feed the rivers which flow down to irrigate the vine-
yards and the fields,
Spreading our benediction over the plains and cities
Where pullulate the restless sons of men, the voice of
whose discontent
Riseth like to the buzz of wasps into our peaceful dwelling
place.
We ever seek to draw men hither, that they may repose
Their weary bodies on our vernal breast, and find the
peace
That only we can give, wrapped in the calm of wisdom.
From out our heart healing we pour into their veins
poisoned
By the exhalations of their world; we cleanse them with
our living breath.
Bathed in the aura of our love, wrapped in our silence
Where there is nothing to distract the mind, the soul can
speak,
And thought and aspiration can give birth unto their
most holy powers.
For know O man, O seeker, that upon these our heights
When thou hast risen so far, and shaken off the fetters
which bind thee still to denser earth,
To the enticements of the destructive fires of passion,
To the flowing waters of thine own desires,
There shalt thou find the Holy Ones
Those who, having trod the paths of life and learned all
it can teach,
Have earned the right to keep themselves apart working
from afar,
Detached and calm, undeafened by the restless noise of
voices, passions, fears;
Unconfused by the illusory images of Time.
They are the embodied mind, the visible aspect of the
Will of God.
They form the mighty Brotherhood of Love, Great
Seers, adepts, those who have mastered all Know-
ledge and all powers of earth.

Leaders unrecognized of the multitudinous activities of
lesser men,
Firstfruits of perfected humanity—the mirror wherein
man may glimpse himself as he must yet become.
They live on earth, although ye know them not, and
sceptics mock,
And Western knowledge fails to understand their work
or find their hidden dwellings.
Where else should be those Avatars of old, the saints,
the men of genius,
The mighty Thinkers who taught you wisdom and were
to their lesser fellows as men to ants?
Those who brought down for you the torch of Truth to
illuminate your shadow-haunted way,
Think ye that they were swept into some Limbo, to
some unknown star?
Not so. Love, for which they did strive and live and die,
bindeth them to you still;
Will bind them till the last man has become one of them,
reached bliss and liberation.
This is a part of that mysterious Sacrifice of which all
Holy Books throughout the ages tell:
The sacrifice of those who, of their own free will, refused
bliss beyond thinking
To remain with you, protect and guide you until the very
end
When they will be freed through your enfranchise-
ment.
But for ages past while man, rejecting their teaching,
mocking their wisdom,
Casting them forth with indifference or hate,
Sank slowly into the darkness of the Age of Iron,
They had perforce, to dwell apart, hidden within my
fastness of ice and snow,
Protected by my guardians of wind and water,
My rushing torrents and my rocky heights,
Only descending into the haunts of men when, by no
other means,

Could fresh stimulus and enlightenment be given.
But now at last man's ardent cry for truth, rising from
    every side in streams of power
Hath merited a new response.
Already, a fraction, hath the veil been lifted.
Using the devas as their instruments and intermediaries,
They have poured down fresh inspiration to enlighten
    the more receptive among the sons of men.
Conscious, living particles of the Mind of the Planetary
    Lord,
Seeing all as one, the Past, the Present and that which the
    Present shall become,
Aware, through their own experience, of man's utmost
    need,
They only can give humanity the bread and wine its
    starving soul desires.
To the few, their pupils,
Those forerunners who have dared to force their way
    towards the icy heights of wisdom,
Men chosen by them and trained in divers way;
Men who have been tested and proved faithful, who, out
    of the surrounding dark
Have let their light shine forth,
To them have these adepts ever revealed themselves.
And throughout the ages in secrecy have poured their
    wisdom down.
But now in this age of change, more light will be vouch-
    safed,
That by its gleams the path spiralling the mountain side
    can be perceived by all.
Now into the minds of those who have learned to answer
    to the vibration
Of Love without Desire which the Adepts give forth,
And who can breathe the thin airs of this pure mental
    plane;
Who, fearless and strong, will leap the chasm,
Brave the sharp rocks, and like the mountain goat,
Symbol of those who fear no height nor depth,

Climb with sure feet the perilous ways towards the dizzy
    peaks,
Into the heart of these shall power and knowledge flow.
Already, although they realize it not, many are being led
    from plains and cities,
Through jungles, deserts, through waters perilous,
    towards my brooding peaks.
Aye, they will be so led until the end; they will be lifted
    by the strong hands of love,
Towards the sacred heights of Meru, the Holy Mountain,
Into the very heart of the pure Lotus,
Where they will become
One with the Thought Divine,
One with their God,
The Absolute Existence, Knowledge, Bliss.

XII

THE COSMIC MESSENGERS

From interplanetary Space,
From realms beyond the range of finite thought,
Where Time is not and darkness blends with light in
    THAT for which there is no sign or name,
The primordial Sons of Creative Fire project Their will,
Evolving and disintegrating Form throughout the Seven
    Planes,
And through us, their swift messengers, and all our lesser
    brethren,
Even to that being which ensouls the whirling atom,
Guide and direct the currents, vibrations, waves of
    whatever type of force the Plan requires;
Balancing evil and good, darkness and light, in the great
    scales of perfect equilibrium.
For Action and Reaction are the manifestation of the
    Cosmic Law,
And only man blinded by his senses, thinking the Part
    the Whole,
Sees Good and Evil eternally separate—ignoring that
    unity of which all are a part.
Perfect is the Law, evolving all things towards adjust-
    ment;
For each is a facet of the whole;
A myriad particles of fiery life, mysterious sons of Fire,
Are set in swift rotation by the faintest breath;
No sound, no thought, no movement in any centre of
    manifesting life,
But createth a ripple which flows throughout all realms
    of being
To distances so vast man's comprehension reels before
    such possibilities.
In all creation life responds to life.

Each centre of the indwelling life draws to itself by its
    own mysterious individual magnetism
What it doth need for its expansion.
As the mighty forces sweep in cyclic pulsations, dynamic
    energies,
Upon man's little world, uniting all in the One,
So doth the microcosm of man's body respond; each of
    his atoms
Recognizing unfailingly in the majestic choir, its parent
    note.
From stars, from planets, from energy generated
Within the mysterious centres of the Zodiacal Signs,
Man draws his substance; gathering in the particles he
    needs,
Building throughout his life by act and thought, atoms
    of energy.
Which, after his death, will latent lie until he calls them
    forth to re-incarnate in him,
That he may reap what he hath sown.
And in like manner doth every living thing
Reflect the impress of planetary powers,
Transmutes them or receives from them the fatal impulse
    of its doom.
There is no separate existence; the same Breath vitalizes
Even those Nameless Ones into Whose minds the Creator
    reflects His will;
For e'en the greatest must receive and must transmute
    mysterious forces
According to the same Law as man in the development of
    the rhythm
To which all things from the dull earth clod to the
    remotest star
Eternally revolve.
This Law is the Universal Key.
They, Beings of awe-ful magnitude, guard for you the
    doors
To that dread mysterious Centre whence powers from
    the Unknown

Will, at the appointed hour, flow in upon your world.
Aye, even now the change draws near!
Another Race, Sons of Aquarius,
Seek for themselves a dwelling-place upon the earth,
And for their work new powers are requisite.
The sacred Doors are opened
And we, Spirits of the far realms of space,
Are bidden now pour forth this new life in Cosmic
    energies as yet unknown to man
And bring to him the message of the Spheres,
Revealing mysteries until now shrouded and concealed.
Through us shall man be given the sacred Words;
Through us, who stand upon the whirling circles of the
    Seven Spheres,
Who watch ever for the Sign; wait for the sacred
    Note,
Who live to create according to the Will of HIM who
    made us,
Will sound forth the call to man to watch and wait and
    serve with us.
But each man hath freewill; he may refuse to work
    toward perfection.
He may choose to breast the current; to endeavour to
    stem the tides of God;
He may oppose his puny will to the great will of love
    which urgeth him ever
Toward that union wherein he will find the consum-
    mation of all his visions, all his aspirations.
He may fight on, blinded by his dream of separateness;
Knowing not That which he is;
Warring against phantom hosts—his own delusions;
Beating his fists against the dank walls of the prison
    house
Which he himself hath builded, when upon his right
    hand,
The door to liberation standeth wide.
The God within will wait; He knoweth Himself inde-
    structible;

When the man turneth toward the light, He will be there
    to lead him forth.

Aye, when man desires at last to unite with the divine
    will,

To play his part aright in the stupendous symphony of
    Cosmic Ideation;

When he would learn the secrets of the stars, the ebb and
    flow

Of planetary waves which, like the sea, dissolve all
    things into their elements;

When he would know how he can rule his own destiny
    through perfect comprehension

Of universal Law, and learn to vibrate to the highest
    chord alone,

Blending in perfect harmony all conflicting elements;

When he desires to see and comprehend the infinitely
    small, the infinitely great,

And how he himself may balance these two extremes
    between which he now hangeth helplessly,

Caught within the web of his own ignorance;

When he would learn to use the elements, drawing on
    powers which in him latent lie,

Without knowledge of which the scientist will seek for
    Truth in vain;

Then he must turn to Them Who Know; and putting
    his pride of intellect,

His personal desires, his blind allegiance to instruments
    of finite sense humbly by,

Ask that he be shown the way to higher wisdom; that he
    be trained and disciplined anew,

That all his faculties be enlightened so that he may
    glimpse truth,

No longer with the vision of fallible human mind but with
    the clear sight of Eternity.

But only through seeking out the Ancient Way, wherein
    the sages of the world have trod,

Can man hope to regain the knowledge and the power
    which he,

Through abuse in ancient, forgotten days did for-
    feit;
When because of his pride and destructive might, the
    Word went forth
And out the fair garden where with us, Powers of the
    Elements, he wrought,
Wielding our mighty forces, hearing the great harmonies
    of colour and of sound,
Passing at will into the higher spheres of intuitional
    perception,
He was driven into bitter exile, into the dark of the
    limitations of that ignorance
Wherein still he wanders, blind and dumb, lost in the
    mists of separateness.
Only when he hath learned to control emotion, harnessed
    his personal will,
Only when it hath become impossible to him ever to use
    our powers destructively,
When through selfless love alone he doth desire to lift the
    veil from Truth,
And like unto us will evermore strive, work, exist
According to the Will of the One Lord of Life,
Can he be re-united consciously to that Son of Light
    which is himself.
Then will the final veil be torn aside,
Then will he behold the supernal glory of what he is,
Not darkly any more—but face to face;
The which beholding, he will himself become
The Light, the Life, the Truth, the Way.